10 HOURS

TO

MEXICO

By: Junior Love

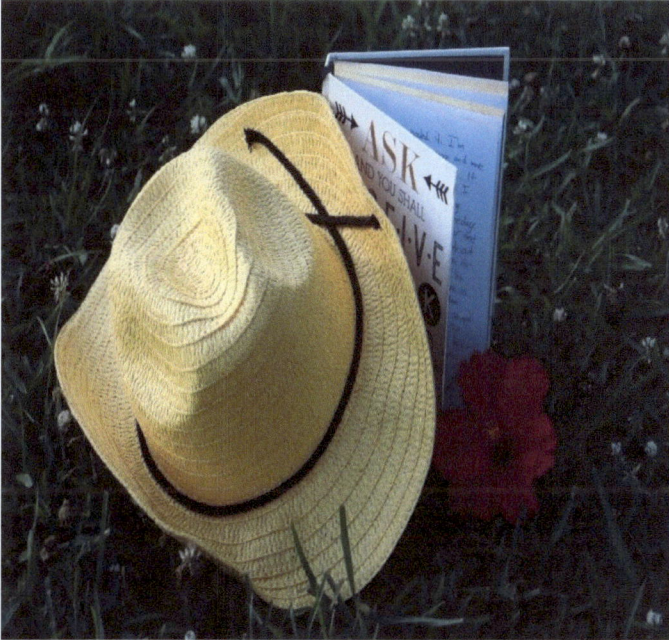

The journal I wrote in to heal my heart.

The Beginning

I'll always remember the day I messaged you
September the 30th
stained with your existence.
Neither a good thing or a bad thing.
Neutral

I recall it like it is
I found you
And you found me

Instantly wondering
Mutual interests inquiring
Casual conversations ensuing

Only over words
Yet never spoken
Finding and realizing distance

The distance of 10 hours
683 miles to be exact
From Monroe, Louisiana
To McAllen, Texas

One could only wonder
Who'd think of that?
Who would be okay with that?

Still we remained in contact
Curious minds wondering
Sexual tensions teetering

Only in our minds
Never expressed openly

This is the beginning

Our ride
From bliss to destruction
Hurt to healing
And ultimately
Growth.

The Texting Game

Responses keep me going
We find that we have lots in common
Not too far in age
You twenty-four
 I twenty-three

Happily, we converse
Through electronic devices only
Feeding off tidbits of information
Gravitating towards the big flakes
Quite like fish

There is beauty in getting to know someone
As we exchange words
Slowly, like a dance
I text, you text

Then... Nothing
I wait...
And wait...

Maybe again, tomorrow.
Slowly, like a dance
A constant reminder
Of the distance that separates us

There is no dinner date
This is different
Communicating through time and space
Through phones and electronic waves
The waves picking up on
our subtle textual flirting
Or maybe it isn't flirting
Maybe, it's just me.
I'll know for sure
Maybe, tomorrow.

Complexation Conception

Big brown eyes
Sleek black hair
A wide, but curvy chin.

Chiseled perfectly to match your face
The nose of a man who has smelled too much,
But not long enough to create distortion.

Thin, but fit and in shape.
I appreciated your smooth skin
The way it glowed
too from within.

Hard working man
You didn't lack in physical strength
It piqued my interest.

Identical twin
Fighting to be your own person
I respected that

Working to be a writer
An author, telling stories
I supported that

A complex person, you are
And I was wrapped up
In all of it.

Long Distance Potential

Experimentation begins fueling my excitement
Knowing the scarcity of openly gay men in my area.
Gay men willing to take a chance
Willing to be free
Along with me.

My love interest is in a predicament much like mine,
at least that's what he tells me.
Conservative family, living in a town of liberals
Catholic, with a dash of hypocrisy

This doesn't deter me
I'm used to hearing the same damn story
One of young gay men and women being oppressed
By their very own family

Those are the least of my concerns
I obsess over distance
The road
The travel
We haven't crossed those barriers
Or discussed those meetings
And yet I ponder

They say that long distance relationships
are set for failure.
But I take chances
Always being told
That for L - O - V- E
Anything is worth it
Who knows where roads may lead
Figuratively, or literally.

Fish O' Plenty

We've been texting back and forth
Quite some time now
I'm getting anxious, impatient almost
At first responses were quick
Now they wane back and forth

I wonder if I'm a bother
Ideas float in my head
Two months and I've yet to hear your voice
Could you be a fake?
A catfish as they say.

I realize that this just won't do
Written words can only tell so much
I need to hear your voice
It's a shame we just can't touch

I gather your attention
Remembering that the internet has its ways
Skype! Of course.
 I've found my way
Invite you for a session
Now it's time to play

All through the night we laugh
Finding that we have even more in common
Seeing you in action through pixelated motion
Family wondering what's all the commotion
They don't see what I see on the screen

Talking about our dreams and aspirations
The stars and astrological inspirations
We looked to the sky for information
Communicating with each other in elation

Comfort in the fact that we felt safe
Safe enough to be ourselves
We've created a space
A space where no one else can tell

We imagined ourselves together
Meeting for the first time
Staying up late and wondering
How we'd spend our time

The one location that stood out
The beach
It was from that moment that I knew
The beach would be where we would share
Our first kiss

I'm not sure if that's how you planned it
I'm not sure if you even knew
I did however, and that was cool
Didn't want to scare you off too soon.
It's cool to communicate with someone
Who shares ideas like we do

Openly talking
Mind freeing conversations
Free from consternation
We connect

Signs, Or blinds?

I started seeing signs that pointed to us being
together
Obsessing over the little things that made me
wonder
Will this happen? Will we meet?
Or will this just get me down like all the other men
I could never meet.

Billboards, TV, and pop cultural references
All of them giving hints
I wish I could break from this
I never saw or knew of the town McAllen
And now it's all over,
replaying in many instances.

Over here and over there
But never too much to make me scared
Sometimes clear, others vague
I wish I didn't feel so damn insane

It's like a movie with foreshadowed scenes
A giant untold mystery

Mr. Smiles

I gave you the nickname and you wore it well
I called you 'Mr. Smiles' and you swore it to hell

I loved it, I really did!
It suited much your cheery grin
Even though I knew often
It was all just pretend
But, if I was forced I'd give it a ten.
Your smile captured the essence of the rising sun
It often would show while we were having fun

A little cliché, maybe a lot
It's just what I saw, and lot what I like.
So I'll flirt a few times just to make you laugh
Give me that smile again and make it last!
If only for a few minutes
Then you may relax.

Out! The figurative closet!

The time was approaching.
Finally, we reached upon an actual date.
March 11th, for spring break.
I was excited
I secretly wondered if you were too.

We had been communicating
for many months now
The only thing stopping us was time

Minutes became hours
Into weeks into months
By now, I was beyond ready
As ready as I'd ever be

Discussing our closest friends
And when we'd introduce them
The inner workings of our lives
And how they could co-exist together
Things slowly began to intertwine
Giving way for new beginnings
By this point, you already felt
Like a boyfriend to me

I remember taking my mother and father
Out on a dinner date.
Introducing the idea of a new romantic interest.
One that was far away, living in a border town.
You called it Little Mexico.

I knew how uncomfortable my dad felt about my
sexuality for years,
It was one of our clashing points in my youth for
many years.
It created a barrier of communication
that discouraged us from being open.

Deep down for years, my father knew I was gay.
I just don't believe he knew how to say it.
He didn't really know exactly how to support me.
He tried though, the best way that he could
But I pushed forward anyway.

I built up so much anticipation and anxiety over burgers.
At the table, waiting until the meal had been finished to
open my mouth.
My mother had nudged the conversation as she already
knew what we were here to discuss.
And so, I say it

"I'm seeing someone... but he lives 10 hours away"

My father perked up, and in an emotional moment tears
fell from his eyes.
I grabbed his hand with an unknown confidence
told him that it was all okay.

"I'm just so happy for you!" He sobbed through the tears.

Years and years of pent up emotion.
I don't think I'll ever forget that moment.
I'm not sure that what we went through in the younger
years of my life had suddenly disappeared.
I was just sure that I had entered a different stage in my
life
One of inner acceptance and independence.

I was no longer afraid of my father.
The one that appeared stern and cold
The one that I thought would never accept me
The one that showed just a bit of emotional sensitivity
But never enough
Never for me.

I had faced all of my fears

told him that I had a potential partner.
I knew then that I had grown.
I had become a man.

Into the night!

Finally the day had come.
Things were ready, set in place
I got all packed up
And ready to go

My trip across the state line
Barely containing my excitement
I'd finally get to see you 'Mr. Smiles'

I said goodbye to my family and friends
I looked at the road
I was ready, I was ready to go.

Hopped in my car
Took off into the night
I reminded myself
It was only 10 hours to drive

2 Hours in
You call to keep me company
We joke and laugh
While I make my way to you
Enjoying your voice as it comforts me
Driving on the highway
No one can touch me

3 Hours in
Something gave in
Engine light lit
And fear began to sink in
"I knew it!" I say

It's dark
I have no clue
of the people, out this way
I place you on hold,

Stop
in a dark place

Call a best friend
A sister to me
Living in the UK, her fiancé in Texas
She knows the plight
The plight of long distance relations
You could say she taught me things
Things I needed to know

She says "Don't you worry,
It'll be taken care of, ya' know?"
I submit and cry over the phone
Thankful for her greatness
Appreciating her, so.

Coincidentally
Her fiancé is close
It's a miracle, or maybe
No coincidence at all.

I am grateful, I am thankful.
He comes to the rescue.
Alternator problems.
A piece of junk.
I should have known
This Volkswagen Passat of 02'
Would put me through all this trouble

But he too says "Don't worry, It's taken care of"
He houses me in his home
Taking good care of me
Teaching me the importance of friendship
Making sure that I am well!
I appreciate the good friends
The good friends that I have.

I return to the road

Returning to my mission
To visit you 'Mr. Smiles'
After my little intermission

And finally
10 Hours in
I arrived
Exhausted
Weathered
A bit stressed
A little late

I couldn't contain
The excitement of joy
The joy that was made

"On the road... To finding a friend. Lost, but yet again"

We meet!

I rested the day I arrived
I was much too tired to meet with him
He remained on my mind that entire night

All the virtual conversations came to play in my
mind
I was ready
Ready this time

We met for the first time
Meeting with a hug
Then a gaze in the eyes
Oddly enough
It felt so right

Awkward tension easily dissipating
Because we had felt each other's skin
We sat over our first meal
Making conversation and stealing glances
Realizing that this was easier
Than what we had made it to be

I still remember the piece of food that he had
between his teeth
Being too scared to point it out
I rubbed my own teeth to make him see
And boy was his smile brighter than behind the
screen
We continued our journey to creating
Our own vision of our lover's road to be.

I had a gift for him
One that I prepared
I knew he would love it
I knew he would care

And so I prepared to give him his gift
Nothing too big
But a welcome to him
A gift from me
A gift to him

Gifts From the Soul!

I gave him a deep green gift
One with a message and to create with
It was a journal of his favorite color
Within the message
Sentimental value

A message to follow his dreams and aspirations
To give into the small inkling of inspiration
Be taken on a journey
A message that I would continue to support him
Regardless of what would happen between us

I still hold true to those words
I wish him no harm
Wondering if he revisits those words
I know the power of words

Here's to hope
Hope that powerful words create the inner fire
The fires of everything that he desires

The second gift a hug
A hug so powerful it shook the world
Transferring the warmth of my heart
To make sure when he thinks of me
He remembers my soul

A hug that protects even from the darkest of
wounds
Bringing him peace when all things be
misunderstood
These gifts I left to him
Even though they were not to keep him
I hope that they instilled faith to a man
A man who believed that love could not be
Due to the circumstances of his upbringing

That believed that he himself was not worthy
Worthy of a healthy love
I hope that it brings him to someone
Someone who could love him
The way he needs to be.

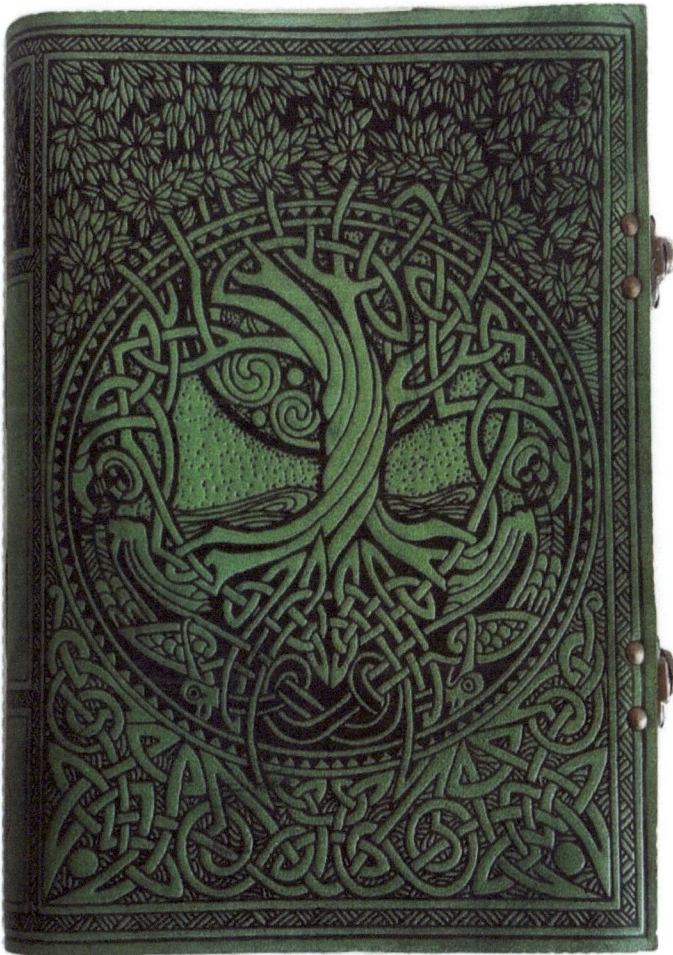

The Beach

We chose a cloudy day for the beach
A bit windy and cool, but I enjoyed your company
Together with your brother and his girlfriend
It was a blast, and it felt so right then.

We stocked up the car with lots of drinks
Ice in the cooler, alcoholic treats
Drove to South Padre Island, hand in hand
Finally, we got to the sand.

The wind blew, and cool air brushed our skin
We sat in the sand, staring and looking from within
I touched your leg, you looked at me
Wind blowing your hair and the ocean
synchronizing

All of us together, having a great time
We played some drinking games passing the time
Moments seem to slow, and it was finally then
We turned to each other and had our first kiss just
then

The wind grew stronger, helping us engage
More kisses blew with the wind, and the ocean gave
way
It was like our own little moment where no one else
cared
Flowing with the motion of our emotions which took
its shape

I'll never forget those moments, even though
Time seemed to slow, they escaped us like sand.
Slipping through the cracks of our hand

I'm grateful for that moment.
I promise, I won't forget it

It's unfortunate however
That I think you'll regret it.

Back and forth on the idea of telling your parents
You swayed just like the wind on the beach
I promised that I was there for you, you didn't have
to worry
Which ever decision you chose, I would be there for
you.

One moment telling me you will, the next telling me
you wont
You couldn't, but you could.
You can, and you can't
Maybe, maybe not.

I grew tired of the swing of back and forth
Although, I didn't really want you in any trouble
I pushed you to tell your parents
I grew weary of back and forth
In and out
Up and down

"Tell them" I pleaded
"I'll have your back" I insisted.

This caused our first spiral
You weren't ready and you knew this
Emotionally you were tired and mentally pushed
against a wall
I didn't mean to do this to you, but your panic sent
me for a rush
I didn't know what this meant for us.

The Bard

We took it upon ourselves to meet one of your
friends
I couldn't wait to meet her after all of the things you
said.
After our experience at the beach, things felt a bit
more connected.
We felt more synchronized than ever before.

On our way there, we played music of all kinds.
You the driver, and I the DJ.
Playing classics and some of our favorites.
We discovered our tastes in music to be quite
familiar.

We approached your friends house,
there I was.
Finally, feeling part of your own little world.
No longer did it feel like we were separated.
Separated by the distance caused by the cables of
our internet providers.

After all the formalities of meeting your friend were
through, we sat around together.
We told stories, shared experiences, we sang.
Her on guitar, and the rest of us on vocals.

There was a spark in the air.
A connection that can only really be understood by
individuals who seem to fit together in this
everlasting puzzle of the world.

Pieces that seem to fit, but not quite.
Filling in different parts of the same puzzle.
Overall, together, we felt like a unit.

We enjoyed the rest of our night.

My Own Doubts

There's a feeling that I believe many of us can relate to.
It's one we'd rather not address.
A feeling one knows, when they almost reach
A breakthrough.

You get so close to the finish line but stop dead in your
tracks.
You promised yourself you'd never go back and find
yourself in the same spot.
You finally come home only to find an eviction notice at
your feet.
You remembered to breathe, only to find yourself
grasping your chest, back down on your knees.

Yes.
The feeling of safety being ripped
right from underneath you.

I was beginning to feel that things were going a bit too
well.
You knew all the right things to say.
At least, I thought you did.

It felt comfortable in the moment,
but in the back of my mind I wasn't always sure.

And now,
The beginning of my doubts.
They grow
from the healthy and plentiful seeds that you planted.

Your Reality

I started to see your situation in the truest light.
Although you were close to your parents you had lots of
fights.
Those fights were very much about your sexuality and
who you were as a person.
At first, I wasn't sure but when I confirmed it with you, I
knew.

While I told my parents about you
I wondered how you would begin to even tell yours about
me.
Truthfully, I just wanted you to be okay with your
decision.
I knew very well the issues of parental acceptance
how it trickled down to our brains
and mentally affect us.

You always assured me that we'd be okay.
You didn't feel your parents would get in the way,
that it wouldn't affect the feelings you had for me.
I took you for your word.
Probably a mistake.
No.
A huge mistake.

Façade of Smiles

Difficult are the ones who smile through the pain
It makes it harder to see past the rain
The rain that ensues inside one's heart
Rather the rain that flows from your own heart

Inklings or impressions of your hurt
They can be seen through your smile
Bringing traces of feelings
Indentations of memories
Troubled past and identities
At times called trauma

I felt your pain just as you did,
when your battle was fought with the ones you
loved
And though you hid it, through the smile you gave
I saw through the façade of your smile

At times, feeling as if you lied to me
Other times, remembering you were lying to
yourself

I just wanted once, for your smile to give
The contrast, brightness, or strength hidden
In the potential it gave when we first met

For you to be yourself
To know that you deserve to love
And be loved

But that isn't easy
I know it isn't
It never will be

At the very least, not for you

Unconditional Love

You were raised by two demons
A mother and a father
Conditioned by the religion they gave their lives to
At least that's how I saw it

Always interrupting the flow of your creativity
A writer was it?
Angry that your soul represented the colors of the
rainbow
An embarrassment to the family name
At least that's what you told me

How could a parent detest their child?
Excuses for scorn
Convictions of hate
Sure, there was love... Somewhere
It wasn't unconditional however
It never came without a fight

How could a parent deny their child from their birth
right?
The right of becoming who they really were meant
to be.
You became a beacon of disgust
Thankfully, they had a twin to profess

One that wasn't gay like you
As far as we knew
One that didn't embarrass the family
Quite like you do
What a shame!

A shame that even though I saw a beacon of light
within you,
somehow you never quite could see that light
yourself.

Always being pushed to the back
Going unnoticed while you lacked
Qualities of the man they wanted you to be
Qualities of the man I knew you could be

Religion pushed you away
I pulled you back to me
And yet, that wasn't enough

You were afraid to love
All your life you had to fight for the love you wanted
to receive
Easily the love I was willing to give to you
Yet you were stuck
Caught in the web of your parent's wishes
Become a psychologist?
But what about the writer you wanted to become?

I could easily see how uninspired you became
To have such aspirations
But be locked down
Be locked away
Constantly in fear of disappointing them

You looked for the approval
 you knew you'd never receive
I'm still not sure
how you'd ever think that would work

Bargaining your dreams
so that they could love you
So that you could love yourself
And in turn be able to love someone else

My love,
It never works that way.

"The truth in your feelings, exposed. Sinking into the water like the flower you chose"

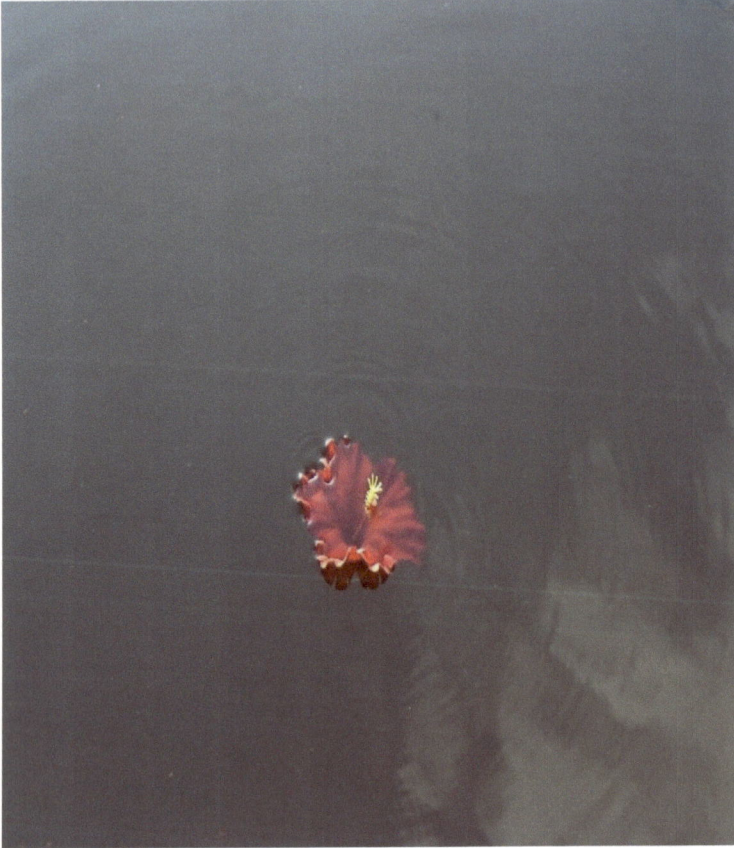

Olive Garden Conversations

What a night
I remember the thought
blaring in my head
"He's going to break up with me"

And yet, I drove to the Olive Garden
As we sat discussing our problems
You had issues, you said
Something about how I liked to solve them

You looked me in the eyes
Me noticing
Your breathing slowing
Swallow hardened in your throat

The waiter comes to interrupt
"Water with lemon please"
She leaves
You resume

"I just think that you're more invested in this than I am"
As the words shatter from your lips
I glance back at my cold glass of water
Should I throw it?
If it hits his face, will he even know it?

Were the 10 hours of destination not enough?
When I was there for him was it too much?
I remember how much the time slowed
Thinking back on all the things I did to show

To show you how much you meant to me
Even when you didn't mean much to your family
A gay man lost in the depths of insanity

I had to stifle a laugh of intensity coming from
within me
A laugh of delirium

Then, the worst of all
Your energy changed
I remembered the way your warmth
Fizzled to the cold of the deceased

Is there a zombie sitting in front of me?
You were no longer the same person
No beautiful smile, no cute face,
No care in the way the that you looked at me

I didn't recognize the person in front of me
Fear rising in my throat
You're not the same person...

The bill came, but your spirit left
As the restaurant closed
We paid the check
It was done
We were done

"You live in America. Wishing to live as free as the country prides itself to be. Confined by the shackles of your elders, and the prison of your mindframe"

Introspective Punishment

I don't understand why I allowed you to drag me
this far down the road with you.
If I knew it'd get this bad I would have left you
when we were truly through
Instead, I stayed and played the friend.
Hoping that someday my feelings would subside
And we'd be cool

It was a bad idea and I knew
I just couldn't put you aside because I felt
I'd be putting you down, casting you aside
And letting you down like your family would

I didn't want to be the bad friend
The one that isn't there when he's needed
But instead, I created a monster.
I allowed all the feelings I had roll into something
disastrous
I didn't know how to end it
I didn't know how we'd stop it

I still checked my phone daily
Making sure to respond back to messages promptly
Being sure to address your concerns
But I started to notice that this was all on your
terms.

Sure, you asked if we could be friends.
But you pulled the trigger and ended our
melodramatic and romantic mess.
Why did I agree to be friends?
When I wasn't ready to not be less than lovers, part
of sin.

We communicated as if nothing had changed.
For months pretending things were the same.
It tore me apart

Even though I was miles away
Months of this nonsense had come to pass
Before I truly realized that this wouldn't last.

We couldn't pretend to be friends
When we acted as more than friends
And then it was my turn with the gun in hand

To pull the trigger and end this mess
And before I did I said it best.
"I love you"
But the words landed on deaf ears
The deaf ears of someone who couldn't love,
much less receive it
Deaf ears and a mute heart...

The phone clicked off and then began
The healing and the growth of my own heart.

HOME

It's been a long journey
I'm finally throwing in the towel
The music is slowing
Quietly winding down
The twists and turns
While they burned
At least I learned
Never to take love
And not give in return

Don't get me wrong
I'm sure I loved you
Don't get me wrong
I'm sure I did
Don't take this the wrong way
Though I'm sure you will
But right now
The only thing that makes me happy
Is the sound of comfortable familiarity
Despite all of my disparity

All I know
Is that it feels so good to be home
Between my sheets
What's underneath
Is the ghost of what was once?
You and me
It's never going to be the same again
That's okay
Because all I know
Is that it feels so good to be home
It's been a long way down
Smiles at first
But now I frown
You used to make me happy
But now you're bringing me down

Where did I go wrong?
Did I take all the love?
And forget
To give in return
Now I returned
Home, at last.

Aftermath

Bitter I became realizing things wouldn't be the
same
I started to see that I couldn't pick up the phone to
call
And text you again

Failure is what I felt.
Knowing this would be difficult
But not to this level

Played back in my mind like movies
Were the times we shared while I had my visit.
All of the laughs
The kisses
The good things shared between us
In such a small frame of time

If only the mind let us travel back to specific days
Allowed us to truly relive those memories
That's how I felt, that's what I wanted
It's just no longer how I feel.

I quickly had to realize that I was doing myself
harm
Self-harm in the emotional sense
Scarring my emotions with the same images
Playing over and over in my head

Our kiss
My gift to you
The eye gazes
The emotional intimacy

But that was gone now
Now I had to pick up the piece from the moment
The fatal moment that I pulled the trigger

I had to realize that things would get better
I would heal and I would learn
Learn to love again

Slowly, yes.
Stronger and Harder yet.
Love that I deserved
Love that didn't' cause emotional shut down
That was going to love me in return

I did not deserve a conditional love
But an unconditional one.
Detaching myself was the true first step
To the genuine source of love
That I still hadn't received yet.

Waxed Love

It is okay to open your heart
And receive the wonders of love.

When your heart breaks,
the blood that runs through your veins
will mold a heart anew.

The pieces that were once softened,
they too will harden again
like a candle made of wax.

When all the pieces fit together again,
your heart will be ready
to venture the world.

At times, your heart will break,
you will return to the beginning of your process
and start again.

An everlasting process
that only strengthens
as time goes on.

Do not be afraid to open your heart.
You will learn
that with each heart break
builds a stronger heart,

Which leaves a stronger heart
for someone who truly deserves
your love.

10 Hours to Mexico

I traveled 10 hours to Mexico
Give or take, didn't know what I would find
Came expecting to find love but that wasn't on his mind
Instead I found broken a man

Full of denial
Wishing he could be anything
Anything, except what he was wanted to be
Pushed into corners by his supposed supporters
Trapped into loneliness, fooled by orders
Orders given to him by family and friends
again, and again, he struggles to bend

To give into the will of others
Trying to find peace and happiness
He struggles to gain acceptance of himself
By seeking it through acceptance of others
Beautiful on the outside, but broken within

"Dear God" he cries "Deliver me from sin"
But God never answered, at least he didn't think so
His mother pulled him aside, made sure he'd believe so
That wasn't what he wanted to hear, it wasn't right
Why couldn't he just be who he wanted to be
Without putting up a fight

It was far too much to bargain with
He knew deep down it wasn't right
And even though, I traveled 10 hours to see him
I couldn't even make it right

These were deep dark issues
Some of inner hate, dysfunction, and familial plight
A family so destined to see him

As a priest to give peace and light
Why should one be forced into a position?
A position that should be holy and bright
If one is not committed
Into the action of being sanctified

Believing that he himself should never love
He tore himself from happiness
And left me in the sun

Deep down, from the very beginning
He knew that we could never be
Just trying to find a bit of joy
Something that he had never seen

I wasn't enough to change that in him
Don't think anyone ever will
It was a sight I hope to never see
Again, as long as I live.

To see a man, so grown
Yet, still a child.
To be at home, imprisoned still.
How much does it cost for a man's freedom?
To be able to live as one should.

Outside of the garden of Eden
Away from the religious spiels
Stuck in a deep dark depression
Using smiles to stave the pain

I see it more as a grimace
He'll never fool these eyes again
I don't wish him bad, I know what he's been
through
I just wish he hadn't taken me for a ride

Still I have the love and respect.
I wish him, happiness and freedom

From the bondage and imprisonment
That only he can free himself from
I learned so much in little Mexico

More than I wanted to know
I learned that I could not save a drowning man
Because he would sink my boat.

As I return home on my trip
I look off into the passenger side
Although you aren't with me
I still feel your presence aside

It sucks that you can't be near me
But it's healthier this time
I know, I must leave you behind
It gets harder realizing each time
And even when I hate you the most
I promise, I'll still be kind.

This is a submission of good intentions
I only wish you the best, a promise for life
I'm sending out some light for you
In the hopes that you'll receive it

I still hold space for you till this day
Nothing romantic, but genuine care
Exactly what you wished for
Something that could never be spared.

I hope you understand some day
That there are people who truly love you
But you'll also have to understand too
That until you reach out your hand

You'll always get less than what you planned to
I'll take this trip and remember it for life
And use these experiences to better myself
For the next man in my life,

that deserves the love I give
Because this trip also showed
How far I'd go to love deeply from within.

DEDICATION & ACKNOWLEDGEMENTS

To my fellow members of the LGBTQIA+ community. First and foremost, I love you. It's hard to formulate the words on paper. Even being the emotional writer that I am, I know that there aren't many words that I can sew together to profess my love for you all. We come in many shapes, sizes, and bring a plethora of talent and inspiration to this planet. This book was written for us! To the very souls who feel left out, abused, sad, and unloved. The ones that feel that they are unworthy of love, unworthy of transitioning, and unworthy of feeling beautiful. I want you to know that you are more than enough to be and do all those things. Don't be stifled by people who clearly can't handle your shine. The very essence of who you are is so important to this world, and I want you to understand that it is essential to your health to always be yourself. I say this mentally, physically, and spiritually. Do not be afraid to cut people out of your life, if it means being able to live the happiest and healthiest life that you can live! You are only granted one life to live. Furthermore, do not sit idle when your brothers and sisters of this community are being attacked. Your stories are important to me, and I will continue to fight to make sure that we are heard, and we are seen. Your beauty knows no bounds. I hope that this reaches you at the time you least expect it and need it the most. We are family. Together we will be as one. Supporting each other through hurdles and most importantly rainbows

I want to thank a few people near and dear to my heart. I no longer speak to the person this book is based on, I thank him too for teaching me about myself. I couldn't have written this book without you. To my lovely and wonderful best friend and sister, Hema. You have no idea how much I appreciate everything you've done for me. Without you, this book would also not have been written. You've been my shoulder to lean on from many miles away. By the time this book is released, you will be married. Congratulations to the both of you! I also thank your husband for picking me up after my car breakdown. Otherwise, this book would have never been created. To my internet pen-pal and virtual best friend, Vashaé. Thank you for leading me in the right direction and listening to my rants. You've picked me up when I was down, and I

will never forget that. You're also a reminder that friends don't need to live close to each other to be friends. Thank you, Monique. Although we have not known each other for very long, I feel like I have known you for quite some time. You've inspired me to pick up the pen and reflected the poet that you saw in me. I won't let you down friend. Finally, to my mother and father, Ronny and Evelyn. I love you both so much! I thank you for believing in me and supporting me to the fullest. You've never let me down. I wish that everyone could have parents as accepting as the both of you.

ABOUT THE AUTHOR

Ronny Smith, Jr. is a creatively diverse artist from New York, New York. His passions include singing, writing, music, abstract art, and conceptual art. Ronny is passionate about mental health and domestic violence advocacy and is currently pursuing a career in social work. When he is not guiding viewers with his Facebook Livestream show, Your Best Friend, you can find him writing emotion-grabbing poetry as Junior Love. Be on the lookout for Ronny's upcoming album *10 Hours to Mexico*.